QUITTING TIME

POEMS BY JACK VEASEY

ACKNOWLEDGEMENTS

Grateful acknowledgement is made to the editors of the following periodicals
in which some of these poems previously appeared: **ASPHODEL, THE BLUE
GUITAR, BONE AND FLESH, HARBINGER: A JOURNAL OF SOCIAL
ECOLOGY, THE PAINTED BRIDE QUARTERLY, PHILADELPHIA POETS,
THE PITTSBURGH QUARTERLY, THE SOUTH STREET STAR,** and
TABULA RASA. "Prayer" is available as a greeting card from Aries Cards,
1130 Church Street, Lebanon, Pennsylvania.

"Quitting Time" and "Winter Oasis" are featured in the travelling multi-media
exhibit "Voice Prints," with accompanying photos by Glynis Berger. This
book's cover photos by Glynis Berger are excerpted from that exhibit, which
has been shown at several locations, including the Painted Bride Art Center in
Philadelphia.

Book design and illustrations by Harry H Long.

Typesetting by Jeanne's Word Center, Lebanon, Pennsylvania.

All poems copyright 1991 by Jack Veasey.

ISBN 1-879294-00-1

Library of Congress Catalog Card Number: 90-72085

WARM SPRING PRESS
P. O. Box 5199
Harrisburg, PA
17110

QUITTING TIME

© BARRY H LONG 1991

Contents

Urban Child Psychology

Give the boy a
broken
window
as a
jig-
saw
puzzle … One day,
he'll
grow
up
to
scrape
the
sky.

© HARRY LONG 1991

Chameleon

A lizard much like
the majority of men, adept
at blending in with backgrounds,
instantly
invisible
like any proper individual,
like any lizard in the business.

Invisible
and voiceless, one
without its brothers makes
a perfect pet.

But gone grey
against a tweed lapel,
the leash it's on
gone limp, the creature
sleeps and seems
to dream, its tiny eyelids
flickering, its torso
twitching.

It dreams of
a mirror, of
a vacant shade of silver
all its own, of
a floating face whose color
is no color ...

of its own eyes
peering back, wistful
and wise, as if
to say, "I am,
I am."

Data Processing

The screen is not a mirror
or a window;
it shows nothing nearly
human
as a movie.
The word "enter"
does not have to do with doors,
and neither do these kinds
of keys.
These keys assign the human hundreds
each a number,
much as in the real world's
prisons.

But this is
a different world, ruled
by invisible gods, disc-shaped,
whispering laws
without sound, flashing signs
in our eyes.
Here the words
"abort" and "execute"
mean nothing
bloody, bitter,
inconvenient. There is a menu,
but there is
no meal.
Memory
is nothing
personal,
no matter how much
there may be of it.
Machines
remember,
but they never
dream.

Neither do we,
after awhile ...
we're much too busy
sitting here,
day after day,
our fingers
blurring
at a hundred miles a minute
in their frantic dance
to save
what can be saved,
what can be saved,
what can be saved.

Creativity

At times
it seems my hands
know more than I do, dancing
nervously, and
words
form in my mouth
as if by magic

I am painfully aware
of how much
nothingness
surrounds me

I touch
nothingness,
and feel a substance
crying to be shaped;
it cries
the way dumb clay
might cry for potters.
Then

the noiseless voice of
nothingness
is singing
in my fingers

my hands
are spinning, I
am spun

I need no drugs
to speak in
tongues

something disembodied
floods my senses, something
coats my thoughts
with flesh

I act
as I am acted
on; I wake

with a shudder
and see what I seem
to have done.

I never understand, or want
to understand
why I am
chosen, why
I choose ...

I live
mainly,
for the miracle
of this.

Three Mile Island Siren

In Hummelstown, ten minutes
from the power plant
now known for near disaster, they've installed
a warning siren: one horn
on a tall pole
that turns
when turned on,
like the blades
of that TV New's 'copter. Its shriek
reminds me of the fifties,
when I was too young to understand
the air raid sirens I've since read about.

That sound, so they told us at first,
means a meltdown or something;
at any rate, a warning
that, unpacked or no, we'd better
run like hell.

The first time it went off
some did just that, in terror, scurrying
like squirrels. Then it was clarified,
belatedly, that daily tests at noon
were necessary. And furthermore, the siren
would cry "fire," the way most sirens do
these days.

The way you can tell
what the scream means
is how the note's held:
if it's not a high note,
if it wavers
and wails less than 15 minutes,
then it merely means
some neighbor's house is burning; good news
by comparison. Oh, perhaps you'll sense some gap between held bre
a mystic's moment in midair,
before the sound makes clear its meaning,

but such things
you learn to live with.

The damage, actual and only damage,
poisoned only Unit Two,
a fever sealed within lead walls; so say
the N.R.C. PR men.

And here and now, in Hummelstown,
where everyone has always been
a neighbor, there's no fallout,
just a feeling...
when someone's charred, smouldering grief
makes us sigh
with relief.

On the Death of Bud Dwyer

A man who lived in public
dies there too. He makes his death
a media event.

He calls a conference
and shoots himself
surrounded by reporters,
cameras rolling.

His death becomes the merest moment
on the evening news.

We are warned to turn away
and not be traumatized;
we are given crisis phone numbers
to call
should imitation beckon us.

But still his final moment
will be shown
while the whole world
is having dinner.

And the world has seen
much worse
and won't stop turning,
even for the merest moment.

It's over in a flash, blink
and you miss it:
the gun in the mouth
amid shouts of confusion,
the fall, one blood drop
on the wall.

Not as graphic
as the gross-out scene in "Alien,"
the average cop-show shooting,

or the battles in Bugs Bunny.
Much less real-looking
than what we're used to seeing.

But the man has made his point.

His death
is the number one story
for maybe a week,
as far as everyone's concerned
except the folks who watch
"Three's Company"
and game shows.

Soon his name
becomes the punchline
in the jokes one only tells
to certain friends,
but will still be invoked
much more than while he lived.

Until, of course,
the next big story
breaks,
as stories do
and all the time,
making a noise more loudly
than when spirits break,
though they too
do that every day -
mostly without
a single headline.

Only those who really knew him
will remember
there was more to it
than news.

Politics

You'll know you're a success
if your assassin
is a man
you haven't
met.

Freak Show

In the parking lot
of the Colonial Park Mall in Harrisburg,
among the bustling bodies at a carnival,
inside the temporary small town made of rides
manned by gruff, greasy men in denim,

you freeze
before a trailer framed by
shrieking painted signs:

MOBILE MEDICAL UNIT
BILLY REEVES IS STILL ALIVE INSIDE
DRUG ABUSE IS DANGEROUS
THIS YOUNG MAN IS A TRAGIC LIVING TESTAMENT
WEAK HEART? THEN DON'T COME IN!
IF THIS EXHIBIT KEEPS THIS KIND OF TRAGEDY
FROM TAKING EVEN ONE MORE BOY, OR ONE
MORE GIRL,
OUR TRIP AROUND THE WORLD WAS NOT IN VAIN

Your friend is horrified
to hear you're curious.
It's probably a fake, he says,
but if it's real, there ought to be a law.
The kid ought to be in a hospital
if he's for real.
But *if he's for real* is the question
that's most on your mind. Unlike your friend,
you've waited years for this - since grade school,
when the freak show at the local carnival
was kept off limits to the kids under eighteen.

You never saw the Alligator Woman
and you've wondered ever since.
This isn't as exotic, but you're tickled
by the tinge of the forbidden,
though the only stricture left
is in your mind. You need to see

to free yourself, to find what's real,
to face whatever fear you feel.
So you defy your friend as if he was your father.

A midget takes your money at the door.
He boasts that he's the one
the signs three trucks away call
the world's smallest man. He says,
"It's two attractions for the price of one.
Now take a long look if you want."
It's clear he means you ought to look at *him*
before you check out Billy Reeves.

Somehow the prospect makes you nervous.
You say no by saying "Thank you," and you enter.
At Billy's door, a small sign warns you
not to try to start a conversation
due to his "unstable mind."
The first things you see
are his eyes. Unlike the midget's,
they don't look as though they know you
or have seen your type before.
They simply see you. Nothing mocking
or mistrustful, only curious,
and not the way you are.
Curious as animals are, empty of words,
staring nakedly. They make you feel
a little hypnotized. You want to lift your hand
for him to sniff, to show you're not the enemy.
Then you remember the bars
and the reason they're there.
You tear your eyes from his, force them
to travel the whole picture.

Other than the eyes, the face has no expression.
Other than the eyes and face, if you ignore the cage,
he looks quite normal: thin, frizz-haired, pockmarked,
in green surgical smock, old jeans,
and dirty white wool socks.
He sits dazed on a straight-backed chair
surrounded by the cage of iron bars -
from floor to ceiling, nine by twelve.
Above his head there hangs
a bottle upside-down: a bit like an IV,
but not hooked to him.

He could be anyone except for those wide eyes.
They ask a question you could never bear to answer,
even if there *were* an answer. He wants something
but he can't remember what, and couldn't say
in any case. To see him search you with those eyes
has made your curiosity much worse. To look at him
can't satisfy it. Now you feel the need to see as he does,
to let go of knowing things, and the desire is terrifying.
There's no other way to know what his reality is.
He is awake, but not conscious. And you, you're asleep,
dreaming this, and you don't want to stay.
No, you don't want to get your money's worth.
He's the one who's caged, but you feel trapped.

You back along the trailer's length abruptly,
watching his eyes follow you. Then suddenly, as if
forgetting you, he tilts his head back
and starts drinking from the bottle … in great gulps,
cheeks puffing like a pet shop rabbit's,
eyes shut like a blissful baby's.
How can his world be so simple, you wonder,
astonished.
Then you hurry out the door.

The midget wants to know
if it was worth it. You tell him
you were totally convinced -
which isn't really a straight answer, though you were.
All you can feel is ashamed, but you don't tell him that.

You tell yourself you didn't go to scoff, only to see.
You tell yourself it doesn't matter
where the money went.

You tell your friend
you wonder how you'd look
to eyes like those, to eyes
completely free of any prejudice.
He tells you you'll find out
on the next ride,

and leads you to
the
funhouse
mirrors.

Why I Love Pro Wrestling

Jake "The Snake" Roberts
drapes Damien - the luckless boa
carried in a sweat-stained canvas bag -
over a man who weighs more
than a Mazzaroti,
and the "victim" faints from fright.
Believe *that*, and there's a bridge
I'd like to sell you.

It's true that this is not
a sport, exactly, that the scripts are not
convincing, that a punch is never
thrown
without a boot discreetly stomped
to fake the impact, that the wounds are
self-inflicted furtively, to earn a rate
like overtime, a practice known as
"red for green."

And it's true that Hitler,
speaking of this audience,
would never have to heave a sigh and say,
"Tough Room."
But the crazed matrons whose placards scream
about the villains' puny genitalia
are *not* handing pensions to some sleazy preacher.
And the Americans are all blond gods,
the Russians shaved-head thugs, like on the evening news
except more openly, without the threat
of swapping bombs.
And the announcer's British accent isn't bad,
considering he's from New Jersey.
And best of all, it makes big liars
of the cynics who have always said
that no-one ever sweats on television.

And the breasts of Abdullah The Butcher
are bigger than Mamie Van Doren's,
and yes, *they*
are real.

Hooker

Hardnailed hand on
ample hip sealed in
red satin stretched beyond
old limits, as her sharp
eyes
scan the steady
stream of
cars

All
nasty sass, all
barter charged with
banter,
she is
true
street
theater

as much a sign herself
as any
neon
word
that lights her
stage, this
corner

'round which traffic
snarls like
lions
pacing in close
cages,

countless
cars

at this ungodly
hour, when
the peak's not

reached it seems
forever, when
the timelock in the mind
locks on
and holds at hot, high
noon - despite the moon,
despite the need for
sleep - till dawn
the netherworld's rush-hour
drives on ...

In her way, she is
much wiser than
her momentary men
will ever be;

she sees
the limp within
the pushy
strut, the bad
nerves burning
cigarettes,
the hands
that shake
with what they toss away or
take:

she has been privy
to the hidden
scars
of many
nameless
strangers, and been
matchless in the
ruthless art of
seeing in
the dark

A threatening victim who'll
fuck, but
will not
be
fucked
with

she moves along
through history, outliving
every law, glistening
symbol
of the world that won't
admit her part in
everything
we
are

Even those to whom
she is a sad statistic or
a dim idea, even those
who merely read of her
existence distantly and on
occasion as
an abstract fact less real than
last week's
headlines,

even those
who fear
their feelings
far too much to even
dream
about her
touch,
all of them
use and
use
and use
her;

she's the negative
from which they are
developed
into pictures fit
for print.

I pass her on the street
each night while
heading home
from work, and I have said
hello
and only meant

hello,
and we've just
known
each
other's
faces, but

I've seen a softness in
her eyes I
think, perhaps, no
businessman could
buy…

and it *is* business, strict
and serious, she's
caught up in and
I
won't
interrupt
her,
but

I often wonder
what she has to
say

Three Prose Poems

He discovers it stings whenever shadows touch his skin. He avoids bars and crowded streets. He sleeps alone. He avoids all shadows but his own, with whom he boxes nightly. He says, "Only when I can hit back, will I let me get hit." He thinks, "Someday I will invent paper that casts no shadow … and pens."

He thinks, "Someday I will write a book."

Twins stand before a man in dark glasses in a park.

One says, "My brother is a good fool; says nothing, does everything. Forty-five dollars, he's yours."

The man in dark glasses ponders. The breeze holds its breath. When he decides, all the pigeons fly away.

He hands one his money and drags the other one away.

The remaining twin counts his money, saying nothing, grinning like a fool.

CHARRY H. LONG 1991

She told her son not to go into the jungle because a lion might eat him. He went anyway.

When she returned to the house, a lion was sitting on the couch, watching television.

She fainted.

The lion padded over to her, and licked her face.

Influenza (a sestina sans tercet)

Yes, the body is a city, with all streets congested,
though the time does not seem busy with the body clock run down.
The neck, back, arms, legs, nose, even the mind are aching,
and for once it is not love or rage that leaves you feverish.
The throat, stripped of all song, is now a mere canal for phlegm,
and all things end no more in death, but diarrhea.

It is the opposite of ordinary: the mouth is free of diarrhea.
No-one speaks of distant wars when his world seems only congested.
Unseen bloodshed seems like trivia compared to spouting phlegm,
and the heart bleeds for no strangers with the heartbeat so run down.
On a better day, the evening news might leave you feverish,
but no heartache can compete with so much concrete aching.

Suddenly you understand old aunties who complain of aching,
though you'd always thought such talk was so much verbal diarrhea.
You swear you'll never let their whining make you feverish
again. How could your love-struck tear ducts have been so congested?
In your weakened state, tears of compassion suddenly run down,
until you get distracted by a surge of phlegm.

Odd, how your semen has the same consistency as phlegm.
You'll think on that in detail after you stop aching.
Perhaps that's why lovemaking leaves a person so run down,
and all those "headaches" aren't psychic diarrhea.
Bored, you ponder this until your mind, too, is congested.
Dazed philosophizing leaves you feverish.

Dazed philosophizing leaves you feverish,
until you fill another tissue up with phlegm.
By now, the bedside trash-can has grown too congested,
so you empty it, and anger joins the aching.
You take this as a sign that maybe you are getting better, but then
     diarrhea
hits you like the truth. You're still too hopelessly run down.

The TV news admonishes, "be patient, and the virus will run down,"
or run its course, or some such something. You're too feverish
to listen. Then you're spared from tales of terrorism by more diarrhea.
If this poem appetizes less than phlegm,
be glad next time only an author's soul is aching.
Lofty poems, after all, are merely tissues for the spiritually congested.

Common Law: A Villanelle

I want a family, but not by accident;
not bound merely by law, or whims of nature's.
I want a family that chooses me.

Blood is not necessarily the bond it ought to be,
as any battered wife or child well pictures.
I want a family, but not by accident.

Through walls, neighbors hear words cruel and meant
to be; the therapist hears tales of mental tortures.
I want a family that chooses me.

I want a friend whose love has not been lent
to meet a debt incurred before my face grew features.
I want a family, but not by accident.

With blood not only in our veins, but on our hands, we see
respect not earned is no born right of any human creature's.
I want a family that chooses me.

Ties that bind but are not chosen may be bent,
but those we tie ourselves can truly be our teachers.
I want a family, but not by accident.
I want a family that chooses me.

Two Sonnets

You still don't know, and I won't tell yet. I
will revel in the innocence of this.
What you don't know won't hurt *me,* and the bliss
of which I'm ignorant is best a sigh
left lingering where longings hide, within
fond fantasy, the place where longings live
the longest. I look on you as mystics in
the state of Grace see God's face, God's forgive-
ness; your flesh, gleaming beyond reaching. But
I know, from what you've told me, of your wound
within, deep, much like mine, the troubling cut
made on your mind by boorish bosses; tyrants called your tune.
We have both been laughed at, left out, lost and poor.
But of this bond between us, I am still not sure.

You, who've seen me through the worst of times, should
know that, when I'm better, *we'll* be better
too. That's why, my love, I write this letter
promising that, in becoming more good,
I'll be, too, more good for you. If I could
I'd be a stronger source already, fetter
no more, liberator. Then together
we could face whatever troubles should
befall us both beyond blunt edges of
benign events. We could be pure pillars holding
up our sky - or be stars, even, you and
I. This may seem brash, such pride unfolding
from a man so lately broken, but love,
what I write, I write with trembling hand.

To A Man Found In A Church

How long
have you been kneeling?

Where once-pure light leaks
down, now
stained, through
glass ...

is it to all these windows
you are
bowing?

Better not to!

Better to find windows
you can see through.

Angels knelt here
once; now
they are statues.

On your feet, man! Ask
outdoors, out
loud;

sing
instead of mumbling to thumb-knuckles!

Sing instead;
for clear light,
and for feathers.

The Life of the Party

On the deck behind John's house
we sat and drank and talked and watched
while a man in a wheelchair
was dancing.

He *was* dancing,
though some wouldn't call it that:
twisting, now tilting,
withdrawing, approaching
the woman he spun with one hand.
To say it was graceful
would really not say how it was -
this grace looked like the kind
religious people mean when they say
"state of grace."
It was summer, and sweat glistened
on his bearded face,
and on his arms and chest,
soaked through his tanktop, drenched his hair ...
but simple sweat did not explain his radiance.
Of all of us - although the one who couldn't stand -
he seemed
the least earthbound,
the one most likely
to unravel everybody's limitations
just by being there among us.

But I was the only one
his dance
arrested:
no-one stopped their conversation,
no-one froze before Sangria reached their lips,
no-one betrayed the awe
I thought we ought to feel.
No, nobody else
seemed especially spellbound by Cecil -
the one man with wheels,

with the hands of a dancer,
with something I couldn't describe, no, not even
to him.

Then came a momentary lull between blared salsa songs
while someone changed cassettes.
Behind our chattering, I heard
birds chirping, sirens, cars, dogs barking in the distance,
all the life we at the party had forgotten,
singing softly all around us.
Cecil rolled back a step
to sit the next one out.
I watched him for another moment ...

breathing hard,
head thrown back,
eyes fixed
on the rising moon,
heart pounding
like the different drum
we heard of in cliches when we were young,
not moving
but still celebrating.

Sometime I have to ask him
what it's really like,
this thing
people call
"joy."

Prayer

Let what I feel fill me
but not consume me;
let me follow what I feel,
but not be forced;
let me become the kind of man
who never clings too hard,
who lets go and yet loves;
let me imagine better worlds,
yet work in this one;
let me touch, and treasure, even
people I can never hold,
and let me learn from all my losses;
let me out, and let me in,
and let me see, and let me be,
a window - maybe broken - but through which
a bit of air and sunlight comes.

Quitting Time

Quitting Time
is not always at five.

Quitting Time
comes when you want
with all your heart
to punch more
than the clock;
when your boss,
ten years your junior, tells you
to shut up;
when you've run out of small-talk,
anyway, and there are only small minds left
in range of hearing, with no time
for listening;
when the choice comes down to salary
or keeping any self-respect at all;
when each weekend feels like furlough
from a war.

Quitting Time
is not announced
by whistles blowing,
but by screams
in your low back, your head,
your neck.

Quitting Time
comes at the end
of that one sleepless night too many,
when you look into a mirror
and, instead of a reflection, see
a shadow.

Quitting Time
won't wait
until you find another way
to pay the bills.

Quitting Time
will have its way with you,
like labor pains, like death;
it will envelop you, grim, loud,
a cataclysm.

And no matter how you grit your teeth
and clench your fists, this thing called
Quitting Time

will save your soul.

Visiting Home

Children who have never even
seen a swimming pool
don't know that playing under fire-plugs
is for dirtballs.

They squeal, dance, feel
squeaky-clean,
although it's cold
and hurts your hands
if you should gather it full-force
into a fountain;
though cops come
to stop the play they say is waste,
and though who owns the wrench
must stay a gleeful secret.

With the old fan's tin drone
rattling through my head,
I watch them through the spinning blades, listen
as fan noise garbles laughter,
know for now
that they can't see me, know for now
they have still been spared
what I see,

wild scrawny strangers
who don't yet know
that they're poor,
who have not learned
to feel the shame,
to mouth the words
we learn by heart,
to taste the taming.

Going Greyhound

She leans on the counter
lazily, her backpack hiding her
from those behind her. It's apparent
that the cashier likes her looks; he smiles,
although she's vague
about her destination.
From the sound of her voice, she's got money
and wants to go slumming, though she affects
the dreamy aura of a flower child.
The cashier believes her,
or seems to; lust
makes him convincing. "Boston's beautiful
this time of year," he tells her, adding
that the Boston bus
won't leave for hours, and he gets off
in fifteen minutes.
They huddle for four minutes more
while the rest of the line,
with a bus to catch, fumes
in disgust, but in silence.
Naturally I am the first to lose it.
"Give us a break, lady.
Why don't you look at the schedule?"
She mutters
and slides away, sheepish.
The cashier glares
and throws my change at me.
The soldier just behind me
slaps my back
and shakes my hand.
Somebody chuckles.

At last armed with a ticket,
I lug my bag down past the lockers
to the turnstile where the guard
argues with someone who will not produce
his ticket. The guard's a new tactic
to weed out the people

who'd slept here, shot up in the bathroom,
or searched here for sex.
"WHAT'M I SUPPOSE' TO DO , MAN?"
shouts the guy ahead of me.
"GET YOUR PERMISSION JUS'
TO TAKE A *CRAP?* LOOK HERE.
I *GOT* THE GODDAM QUARTER!"
I wave my ticket at the guard, who nods.
I jump the rail, run down the stairs.
But I find
the line is stalled, the bus
refueling.

I join with the small mob of people
that waits and waits, growing.
After five minutes,
a tall man in pinstripes
and Panama hat, beard trimmed closely,
approaches me slyly.
"Wanna buy a watch, man?"
he asks. "Gold and quartz …
no? *Only five bucks …*
fuck ya."
The guy behind me
and the couple behind him, it seems,
don't have time for him
either.

But now what fascinates me
is in front of me.
At the line's head, a bag lunch is shared
by a bikerish couple; they're scruffy enough,
and they're wearing what look like club colors.
He's wiry, unshaven, and swarthy;
she's pale, string-haired, heavy.
The look is classic with just one thing
out of place -
he has no arms beneath the elbow.
I wonder if he lost them in a cycle accident.
Tattooed stumps
stick from his sleeveless vest,
each ending in a knob of bone. And yet
he eats his sandwich, spilling nothing,
elbows lifted to his lips.

Then a voice calls out the news
that now the bus is loading, and I'm shocked
to see him pick up all their bags:
a shopping bag, a duffle bag, a flight bag.
Somehow, with only stumps, he scoops them up,
so suddenly it's startling, slings the straps
over his shoulders. Then, not satisfied,
he holds the door for her. His every movement
is a proud, fierce swagger. We all try, but can't stop
staring. On the bus, he lets her
light his cigarette.

The motor starts. All of us try
to settle back, as we each face
three hours at least. But the bus driver, it seems,
is Mr. Showbiz, mugging at his mike
just like a standup comic. We can smoke in the back, he says,
though not cigars or "funny" cigarettes.
As for me, I'm much more interested in sleeping,
though it's hard, with headlights
slicing through the windows
once we've pulled out of the station.
So I pull my baseball cap over my eyes, lay back, and listen
till I find it - a familiar sound
on which to meditate, the most familiar sound
of all ...

the sound of a soda can,
empty,
that rolls
up and down the aisle
soothingly,
soothingly,
all
the
way
home.

Winter Oasis

In the world where I grew up,
there were no stars,
and even had there been,
to look up was not safe,
and even if it had been safe,
I never had the time.

But here, on this wild hill
covered with snow,
hiking while high with friends
though it's late and past freezing,
stumbling, laughing,
I looked up, and looked, and looked,
till my neck ached.

The sky was full
as it had never been before
of pin-sized phosphorescent sequins,
or the suns of distant planets -
facts meant little.
Stars looked so close
I could feel them warming me,
much like these friends
who led me here.

After tonight,
no matter where I walk,
the sky and I
will never be the same.
Now it is safe.
Now I have time.

First Communion

I followed the light
to the spot where it fell
in the hills

I hoped, of course, to find
a person
from another planet,
from a ship that flew
on endless energy

I hoped to hear
a strange voice
speak to me. I hoped,
at least, to find
a place of impact, force,
earth
scorched by foreign metal

What I found, instead,
were merely
cold
and darkness,
those familiar
facts
of
life.

I still don't know why it depressed me
to learn that the light I had seen
was a light from within
my own mind; that the world within me
may well be
the only other world I'll ever see …

What I found, after all,
in the hills, in the night

was myself,
wishing worlds into being,
believing in magic, beginning

a story,
this story,
my story

in my voice, beneath
my
own
sky

Niggerlover

for Cindy Miller

Not just a working-class word,
although that's where I heard it ring out —
off the walls of a working-class world;
not my name, though used
as if it were;
and not the truth —
the truth was more complex:
I loved Jose Martinez,
and I really didn't know
what "niggers" were.
I didn't know the word could be applied
to someone quiet, soft-voiced, shy,
to someone even smaller than most boys our age,
still gentle,
still not hardened by his wounds,
still one to run away from trouble,
still preferring play to danger.

I didn't know the word
was blind to everything
except what met the eye,
that so much hate
could run skin deep
and reach no further.
I didn't know how *early*
poverty could break you, fill you up
with only fear of the unknown.
I feared the ones who used the word —
I knew them, as I did not know
the world beyond the schoolyard's grey horizon.
And I knew Jose
as I did not know them:

Jose, the one dark boy
to go to Catholic school,
one boy
who would not swear, one boy
who had no dad at home
to teach him to talk tough
and beat him, the one other boy
who sang songs and drew pictures, the one other boy
who didn't seem to fit in crowds.

How could he be the faceless enemy
who had left all our fathers ranting?
To me, he was
Jose, only Jose,
the one boy who would be
my friend.

Being white, I couldn't see
how I was serving
as their nigger too,
though neither they nor I
knew why yet.
For the unknown
has a color all its own
even the blind can recognize,
and every shred of difference threatens
when you live in a big world
in which you will always be small.
And those boys, though taller than us,
had already stopped growing.
We felt that difference,
though we didn't understand it.

And Jose would one day
stop his growing, too —
bitten by drugs, sucked dry
of courage. Jose would one day
turn on me and hate me too,
as he'd hate everybody
white.

I would lose Jose
as I would lose
this place I still confused
with the whole world,
this place I sadly called
my home.

I would lose all
except the difference
that drove me,
felt by all, seen
just by some.
I would go alone,
and leave them ranting.
I would learn to love
myself.

In Defense of Daydreams

Once
I shelved books
for a living
in a dusty
library,

and,
with the books,
shelved several
highschool hopes.
Since

then,
I wrote a book;
now,

others
shelve it.

I hope this poem
reaches one of them.

JACK VEASEY'S previous book of poems, *No Time For Miracles*, was published in 1989 by Yardbird Books, Bar Harbor, Maine. His poems have also appeared in many literary magazines in this country and England, and he has presented his work at public readings throughout the East Coast since 1973.

Veasey is also a well-known journalist whose interviews, investigative reports and reviews have appeared in many publications including The Philadelphia *Inquirer*. As a journalist, he has interviewed many well-known cultural figures, among them film & TV director David Lynch, performance artist Laurie Anderson, comedian George Carlin and singer Joan Baez. His other projects as a writer have included stand-up material for comedienne Joan Rivers.

From 1987 till 1991, Veasey was Program Director of the Paper Sword series of cultural events at the Art Association of Harrisburg. In the spring of 1990, he produced and hosted *Verbatim*, a twelve-week Public Radio literary series heard throughout Central Pennsylvania on WITF-FM. He also received a Fellowship In Arts management Enterprise from the PA Council On The Arts, and worked on publicity and proposal writing for the Afro-American Historical & Cultural Museum in Philadelphia. When the fellowship ended, he was hired full-time at the PA Council On The Arts, where he is now a Program Associate in Literature, Broadcast of the Arts, Media Arts, and various other disciplines.

He is one of eight poets featured in *Voice Prints*, a travelling exhibit of photos "of and about poets and poems" by award-winning photographer Glynis Berger, seen most recently at Philadelphia's Painted Bride Art Center where it opened in conjunction with a reading by legendary Beat poet Allen Ginsberg. His poem "Prayer" was just published as a greeting card by ARIES Cards, Lebanon, PA, illustrated by artist Harry Long.

A native of Philadelphia, Veasey grew up in Fishtown, a waterfront factory neighborhood with a large Irish Catholic contingent. He is the son of a security guard and a cleaning woman. After too many years of urban life, first in Philadelphia and then in New York City, he settled in Hummelstown, a Central Pennsylvania small town not far from Three Mile Island.

To book Jack Veasey for readings, contact Mill Street Associates, 37 Mill Street, Boston, Massachusetts, 02122, phone # (617) - 265-3929.